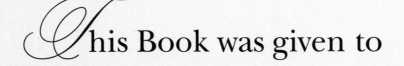This Book was given to

_____

by

_____

on

_____

Best Regards

Recovering the Art of Soulful Letter Writing

Copyright © 1997 by Ben Alex
Idea, design and research by Ben Alex
Printed in Hong Kong
A co-production by
Scandinavia Publishing House,
Noerregade 32, DK - 1165 Copenhagen K., Denmark.
Telephone 33140091
Telefax 33320091

First published in the United States of America by
Abingdon Press
P.O. Box 801
Nashville, TN 37202-0801
U.S.A.

ISBN 0-687-02292-4

Photo & illustration acknowledgments:
Paintings provided by The Bridgeman Art Library, London
Photos provided by Tony Stone Images, London and Copenhagen

Title page photo by Ben Alex

$\mathcal{B}$EST $\mathcal{R}$EGARDS

Recovering the Art of Soulful Letter Writing

Compiled and Edited by Ben Alex

Abingdon Press / Nashville

Contents

Letters are valuable and entertaining in proportion to the wit and ability, and above all the imprudence, of those who write them. Honest letters are more informative, more amusing, more pathetic, more vital than any considered autobiography. Of all documents, these are the most essentially human.

—C. E. Vulliamy

4

MYRON TAPLIN

The Art of Soulful Letter Writing

by Ben Alex

Our spoken words often have a function to perform,
while our soulful letters are meant more for reflection.
The move from function to reflection invites soul into the process.

—Thomas Moore

etter writing is a dying art form. Many of us hardly even write letters anymore, at least not the way we used to, or the way our parents or grandparents did. Since the heyday of personal letter writing during the 18th and 19th centuries, letters as an art form have been on a steady decline.

There simply is not the time to write letters anymore. Modern life has become too hectic and demanding. And even if we do take occasional breaks in our busy schedules, we usually choose for entertainment, rather than the discipline and reflection required by letter writing. We tend to plunk ourselves in front of the television set, or pay a visit to the mall and buy a preprinted card for the special occasion, or we send out fifty photocopies of a Christmas letter, or we just pick up the phone. The price is high. We pay in loss of soul and intimacy within our relationships.

What television did to the art of conversation, the telephone and other electronic wonders such as the fax, photocopier and internet, have done to the art of letter writing. They have stereotyped our communication and freeze-framed our relationships the same way fast food restaurants or ready-made TV dinners have devastated the sanctity of family meals. We no longer live from scratch.

Letter writing takes time. It forces us to pause for reflection, self-examination and self-discovery in ways most modern means of communication do not. A good letter is the most private and honest record there is of how our lives are progressing. Thomas Moore who, more than any other contemporary writer, has helped rediscover the meaning of soul, says in his book *Soul Mates*, "in our letters we are recollecting and conversing with the soul, through both our friends and ourselves." A letter not only tells about the person who wrote it – it reveals something about the receiver and the intensity of the relationship between them. A letter has its own inner life because it is a conversation between two people willing to hear each other out. Letter writing is a way of balancing the debits and credits of life between two people. Their letters are subtotals of a relationship which progresses in intimacy and maturity. Intimacy is the most important ingredient of a soulful letter.

To write a soulful letter requires a change of pace, a shift in attention and focus, a willingness to go beyond a mere transfer of information, and reach for an expression of what is really going on inside of us. Strictly speaking, communicating information is not the same as correspondence; it is a form of commercialism. Intimacy means surrender. It springs from a willingness to open up to our deepest thoughts and emotions, to "expose ourselves to the ghosts," as Franz Kafka, who was also a prolific letter writer, once said. Intimacy insists on a reflection of who we are in relation to our circumstances and experiences, a deeper look. It is daring to "negotiate with ourselves," as Dag Hammerskjöld said, and it means daring to be transparent and vulnerable to the person we have invited into the process through the act of writing. "A man's letters," said Samuel Johnson, "are only the mirror of his heart. Whatever passes within him is there shown undisguised in its natural progress; nothing is invented, nothing distorted; you see systems in their elements, you discover actions in their motives. . . . Is it not my soul laid open before you in these veracious pages? Do you not see me reduced to first principles? This is the pleasure of corresponding with a friend, where doubt and distrust have no place, and everything is said as it is thought." The act of writing a friend or a loved one forces us to be honest and intimate because we are writing *for* someone. We write with a specific audience in mind. This helps us feel at home in our own reflections and theories in a much deeper way than when we write a journal or a poem, or talk on the phone, for that matter. And it requires from the receiver an ability to listen, to feel our pulse and hear our heartbeat. As a result, trust is built. Intimacy grows.

In addition to essence and inner qualities, a good letter must also have form and aesthetic style. It should be "neither unpolished, rough, nor artificial, nor confined to a single topic, nor tediously long," according to Erasmus of Rotterdam. He concluded, "The epistolary form favors simplicity, frankness, humor and wit." This is what is on offer from gifted writers like the ones presented in this book. In their letters they have applied their literary discipline to their personal lives. It is a privilege to read them and in the process, we not only learn how to bring a sense of soul, grace, presence and passion to our own letters and relationships, but also style and discipline. Thomas Moore once said he found it extremely inspiring "to read the letters of artists and writers who reveal themselves in a special way in letters . . . hoping to find a piece of soul revealed in a way different from that in their formal art." So too, we may go treasure hunting and pry into their innermost secrets. Hopefully we will find some nuggets of truth in this vast and varied richness of our spiritual heritage.

We may even feel inspired to write a letter.

JAN VERMEER/GORDON ROBERTSON, 1671

Rainer Maria Rilke

❖

THE SENSITIVE SPOT

Capri, 22 February 1907

I am thanking you with only a few words for your letter, the fifth: I can understand it everywhere and enter with you into your sadness I know so profoundly and for which one can, of course, discover no reason. . . . And yet it is nothing more than a sensitive spot in us, always the same, one of those spots which, when they pain us, cannot be located, so that we do not know how to recognize or treat them in our dumb hurtfulness. I know it all. And there is a joy that is similar — and maybe we ought to get around both of them, some-

Rainer Maria Rilke is one of the best known of all 20th-century poets. He was born in Prague in 1875. His poetry reveals an artist's restless wandering for spiritual truth.

Rilke wrote this beautiful letter to his wife Clara in 1907.

how. I was thinking of that only lately when I had climbed for several days in succession into the lonely escarpments of Anacapri and was so happy up there, so wearisomely happy even in soul. We let both of them, equally, fall away from us, time after time: this happiness, that sadness. We possess neither. And what are we when we stand there, and a wind outside, or a gleaming, or a fragment of bird-song in the air can take us and have its will with us! It is good to hear and see and accept all this, not to be numb to it, but on the contrary to feel it more and more multitudinously in all its gradations without getting lost in it. Once I said to Rodin on an April day full of spring: "How it disintegrates you, how you have to join in the work with all your juices and struggle till you're tired. Don't you feel it too?" And he, who certainly knew in his heart how to take the spring, answered with a quick glance: *"Ah—je n'y ai jamais fait attention."* This is what we've got to learn — not to pay attention to certain things: to be too concentrated to touch with any sensitive side of ourselves those things which we can never reach with our total being. To feel everything only with the whole of our lives — then much indeed (of what is too narrow for us) remains outside, but all the important things are there. ❧

CHRISTOPH BURKI

It is good to hear and see and accept all this, not to be numb to it.

C. S. Lewis is best known for his children's books and writing on Christian themes. In addition to his significant literary works, Lewis also had an extensive correspondence with former pupils, friends and strangers who were responding to his books and lectures. He gave each one the courtesy of a full and personal reply. These excerpts are from letters

There is great good in bearing sorrow patiently.

Lewis wrote to his friend and spiritual "child" Sheldon Vanauken who had recently lost his dear wife. The excerpts are taken from Vanauken's book *A Severe Mercy*, published after Lewis' death in 1963.

C. S. Lewis

❖

TREATED WITH A SEVERE MERCY

It was a strange experience to get a letter from Jean this morning. I return it. You will see that it deals with a problem on which you also wrote me.

The danger is that of confusing your love for her (gradually—as the years pass) with your love for a period in your own past; and of trying to preserve the past in a way wh. it can't be preserved. Death–corruption–resurrection is the true rhythm: not the pathetic, horrible practice of mummification. Sad you must be at present. You can't develop a false sense of a duty to cling to sadness — and when, for *nature* will not preserve any psychological state forever — sadness begins to vanish? There is great good in bearing sorrow patiently: I don't know that there is any virtue in sorrow just as such. It is a Christian duty, as you know, for everyone to be as happy as he can. . . .

One way or another the thing had to die. Perpetual springtime is not allowed. You were not cutting the wood of life according to the grain. There are various possible ways in wh. it cd. have died though both the parties went on living. You have been treated with a severe mercy. . . . She was further on than you, and she can help you more where she now is than she could have done on earth. You must go on. That is one of the many reasons why suicide is out of the question. (Another is the absence of any ground for believing that death *by that route* wd. reunite you with her. Why should it? You might be digging an eternally unbridgeable chasm. Disobedience is not the way to get nearer to the obedient.)

There's no other man, in such affliction as yours, to whom I dare write so plainly. And that, if you can believe me, is the strongest proof of my belief in you and love for you. To fools and weaklings one writes soft things. You spared her (v. wrongly) the pains of childbirth: do not evade your own, the travail you must undergo while Christ is being born in you. Do you imagine she herself can now have any greater care about you than that this spiritual maternity of yours shd. be patiently suffered & joyfully delivered? God bless you. Pray for me. ●➤

There's no other man, in such affliction as yours, to whom I'd dare write so plainly. And that, if you can believe me, is the strongest proof of my belief in you and love for you.

JEREMY WALKER

Emily Dickinson

❖

I AM GLAD YOU ARE NOT A ROSE

Don't tell, dear Mrs. Holland, but wicked as I am, I read my Bible sometimes, and in it as I read today, I found a verse like this, where friends should "go no more out"; and there were "no tears," and I wished as I sat down tonight that we were there – not *here* – and that wonderful world had commenced, which

I find ecstasy in living, the mere sense of living is joy enough.

makes such promises, and rather than to write you, I were by your side, and the "hundred and forty and four thousand" were chatting pleasantly, yet not disturbing us. And I'm half tempted to take my seat in that Paradise of which the good man writes, and begin forever and ever *now*, so wondrous does it seem. My only sketch, profile, of Heaven is a large, blue sky, bluer and larger than the *biggest* I have seen in June, and in it are my friends – all of them – every one of them – those who are with me now, and those who were "parted" as we walked, and "snatched up to Heaven."

If roses had not faded, and frosts had never come, and one had not fallen here and there whom I could not

Emily Dickinson's uneventful life was inwardly dedicated to the task of writing a "letter to the world" about her passion for life. Her writing was a loner's attempt to map the landscape of the soul through poetry. By the time of her death in 1886, she had written almost a thousand poems, all unpublished and neatly stacked in little packets loosily bound by thread. The eccentric "woman in white" was not recognized by the world until the 1920s.

This letter to a friend was written in the late summer of 1856.

waken, there were no need of other Heaven than the one below – and if God had been here this summer, and seen the things that *I* have seen – I guess that He would think His Paradise superfluous. Don't tell Him, for the world, though, for after all He's said about it, I should like to see what He *was* building for us, with no hammer, and no stone, and no journeyman either. Dear Mrs. Holland, I love, tonight – love you and Dr. Holland, and "time and sense" – and fading things, and things that do *not* fade.

I'm so glad you are not a blossom, for those in my garden fade, and then a "reaper whose name is Death" has come to get a few to help him make a bouquet for himself, so I'm glad you are not a rose – and I'm glad you are not a bee, for where they go when summer's done, only the thyme knows, and even were you a robin, when the west winds came,

God is not so wary as we, else He would give us no friends, lest we forget Him.

—From a letter to Samuel Bowles, 1858

you would coolly wink at me, and away, some morning!

As "little Mrs. Holland," then, I think I love you most, and trust that tiny lady will dwell below while we dwell, and when with many a wonder we seek the new Land, *her* wistful face, *with* ours, shall look the last upon the hills, and first upon – well, *Home!*

Pardon my sanity, Mrs. Holland, in a world *in*-sane, and love me if you will, for I had rather *be* loved than to be called a king in earth, or a lord in Heaven.

Thank you for your sweet note – the clergy are very well. Will bring such fragments from them as shall seem to me good. I kiss my paper here for you and Dr. Holland – would it were cheeks instead.

P. S. The bobolinks have gone. ❧

A letter is a soul, such a faithful
copy of the beloved voice
which speaks, that fragile souls
count it among love's most
precious treasures.

—Honoré de Balzac

JAMES DE VINE AYLWARD

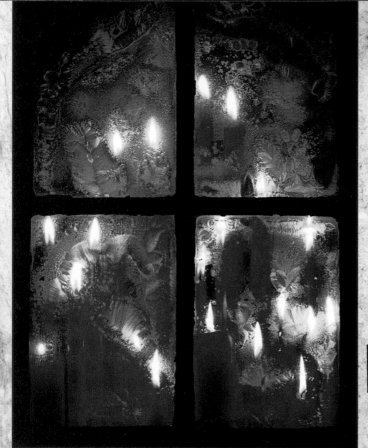

What do happiness and unhappiness mean? They depend so little on circumstances and so much more on what goes on inside us.

Dietrich Bonhoeffer

A GREAT, UNSEEN REALM

I am so glad to be able to write you a Christmas letter, and to be able, through you, to convey my love to my parents and my brothers and sisters, and to thank you all. Our homes will be very quiet at this time. But I have often found that the quieter my surroundings, the more vividly I sense my connection with you all. It's as if, in solitude, the soul develops organs of which we're hardly aware in everyday life. So I haven't for an instant felt lonely and forlorn. You yourself, my parents – all of you including my friends and students on active service – are my constant companions. Your prayers and kind thoughts, passages from the Bible, long-forgotten conversations, pieces of music, books – all are invested with life and reality as never before. I live in a great, unseen realm of whose real existence I'm in no doubt. The old children's song about the angels says "two to cover me, two to wake me," and today we grown-ups are no less in need than children of preservation, night and morning, by kindly, unseen powers. So you mustn't think I'm unhappy. Anyway, what do happiness and unhappiness mean? They depend so little on circumstances and so much more on what goes on inside us. I'm thankful every day to have you – you and all of you – and that makes me happy and cheerful.

Superficially, there's little difference between here and Tegel. The daily routine is the same, the midday meal is considerably better, breakfast and supper are somewhat more meager. Thank you for all the things you have brought me. I'm being treated well and by the book. The place is well heated. Mobility is all I lack, so I do exercises and pace up and down my cell with the window open.

A couple of requests: I'd very much like to read Wilhelm Raabe's *Abu Telfan* or *Schüdderump*. Also, could you fix my underpants so they don't slip down? There aren't any suspenders in here. I'm glad I'm allowed to smoke! Thank you for thinking of me and doing all you can for me. From my point of view, knowing that is the most important thing of all.

We've now been waiting for each other for almost two years, dearest Maria. Don't lose heart! I'm glad you're with my parents. Give my fondest love to your mother and the whole family. . . .

It's as if, in solitude, the soul develops organs of which we're hardly aware in everyday life.

*D*ietrich Bonhoeffer was a German pastor and theologian imprisoned in the Gestapo security prison in Berlin at the time he wrote this letter. He had been arrested because of his involvement in the German Resistance during Hitler's Third Reich.

This letter to his fiancée, Maria, was his last letter to her before his execution in Flossenbürg concentration camp in April 1945.

Marie of the Incarnation

— ❖ —

A MOTHER'S WOUND

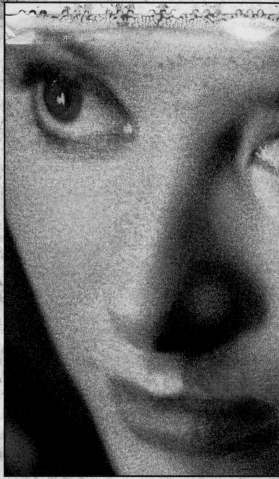

I received your letter and everything in the package when I was not expecting it anymore. . . . You reproach me for a lack of affection which I cannot bear to leave without response, since I am still alive as is God's will. You have some ground to complain about my leaving you. And for myself, I would gladly complain, if

I ask your forgiveness my dearest son; you suffered a great deal because of me.

I had permission from the One who brought the sword on the earth to make such strange separations. It is true that despite the fact that you were the only thing in the world left for me to which my heart was attached, He still wanted to

M arie Guyart, a French nun, became the first French woman missionary to the New World when she arrived in Quebec City in 1640. From there she wrote more than 13,000 letters back to France. This letter was written to her son Claude in 1647.

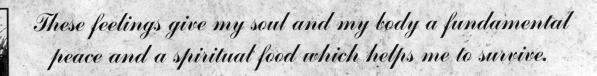

These feelings give my soul and my body a fundamental peace and a spiritual food which helps me to survive.

separate us when you still were at the breast, and I fought almost twelve years more to keep you before it was necessary to part from one another. At last it was necessary to submit to the strength of Divine love and accept this wound of separation, more painful than I can describe to you; this did not stop me from reproaching myself a thousand times for being the cruelest of mothers. I ask your forgiveness my dearest son; you suffered a great deal because of me. However, let us console ourselves in the fact that life is short and that we shall have, thanks to the mercy of Him who separated us in the world, the whole eternity to see each other and to rejoice in Him. . . .

Since my sickness my interior disposition has been characterized by a very particular detachment from all things, so that all exterior things are a cross to me. They do not trouble me, though, for I suffer them by accepting God's orders which put me in a state of obedience in which nothing can happen to me except from Him. I feel in me something which gives me a steady inclination to follow and embrace what I know to be best for the glory of God and what seems most perfect in the maxims of the Gospel, conforming to my situation, everything under the direction of my Superior. I make endless mistakes which extremely humiliate me. . . .

I commit myself to doing whatever He in eternity arranged for me. These feelings give my soul and my body a fundamental peace and a spiritual food which helps me to survive and support all kinds of accidents and all the things, general or particular, which happen to others or to me with a balanced mind – in this part of the world, where it is easy to find occasion to practice patience and other virtues that I do not have... . .

I think that everything that is really good and beautiful, of inward moral, spiritual, and sublime beauty in men, and their works, comes from God, and that all that is bad and wrong in men and in their works is not of God, and God does not approve of it.

But I always think that the best way to know God is to love many things. Love a friend, a wife, something, whatever you like, you will be in the right way to know more about it, that is what I say to myself. But one must love with a lofty and serious intimate sympathy, with strength,

I always think that the best way to know God is to love many things.

with intelligence, and one must always try to know deeper, better, and more. That leads to God, that leads to unwavering faith.

To give you an example: someone loves Rembrandt, but seriously – that man will know that there is a God, he will surely believe it. Someone studies the history of the French Revolution –

Vincent van Gogh

❖

TO LOVE MANY THINGS

Van Gogh, one of the greatest painters ever, stumbled into his art form almost by accident when he was fired as a missionary and began looking for something else to do. His brother Theo, the only person who cared for and believed in the ugly and awkward Dutchman, encouraged him to paint. From the first day that Vincent picked up a paintbrush, he painted with a nervous passion that brought his art to life. Vincent only sold one canvas during his lifetime, but after his tragic death the world realized his genius. A few years ago his small painting entitled *Sun-flowers* was sold at an auction in New York for $53 million.

The following is an excerpt from a letter to Theo in 1880.

he will not be unbelieving, he will see

that also in great things there is a sovereign power manifesting itself.

Somebody has followed maybe for a short time a free course at the great university of misery, and has paid attention to the things he sees with his eyes, and hears with his ears, and has thought them over; he too, will end in believing, and will perhaps have learned more than he can tell. To try to understand the real significance of what the great artists, the serious masters, tell us in their masterpieces, *that* leads to God. One man has written or told it in a book, another in a picture. Then simply read the Gospel and the Bible, that makes you think, and think much, and think all the time. Well, think much and think all the time, that unconsciously raises your thought above the ordinary level. We know how to read, well let us read

then! . . .

I write somewhat at random whatever comes to my pen. I should be very glad if you could see in me something besides an idle fellow.

LELAND BOBBE

Because there are two kinds of idleness that form a great contrast. There is the man who is idle from laziness, and from lack of charac-ter, from the baseness of his nature. You may if you like take me for such a one.

Then there is the other idle man, who is idle in spite of himself, who is inwardly consumed by a great longing for ac-tion, who does nothing, because it is impossible for him to do anything, because he seems to be imprisoned in some cage, because he does not possess what he needs to make him productive, because the fatality of circumstances brings him to that point, such a man does not always know what he could do, but he feels by instinct: yet I am good for somet-

To try to understand the real significance of what the great artists, the serious masters, tell us in their masterpieces, that leads to God.

hing, my life has an aim after all, I know that I might be quite a different man! How can I then be useful, of what service can I be! There is something in-side of me, what can it be! . . .

And men are often prevented by circumstances from doing things, a prisoner in I do not know what horrible, horrible, most horrible cage. There is also, I know it, the deliverance, the tardy deliverance. A just or unjustly ruined reputation, poverty, fatal circumstances, adversity, that is what makes men prisoners.

One cannot always tell what it is that keeps us shut in, confines us, seems to bury us, but, however, one feels certain barriers, certain gates, certain walls. Is all this imagination,

fantasy? I do not think so. And then one asks: "My God! is it for long, is it for ever, is it for eternity!" Do you know what frees one from this captivity? It is every deep serious affection. Being friends, being brothers, love, that is what opens the prison by supreme power, by some magic force. But without this, one remains in prison.

There where sympathy is renewed, life is restored. . . .

We are rather far apart, and we have perhaps different views on some things, but nevertheless there may come an hour, there may come a day, when we may be of service to one another.

For the present I shake hands with you, thanking you again for the help you have given me.

If sooner or later you wish to write to me, my address is, care of Ch. Decrucq, Rue du Pavillon 8, Cuesmes, near Mons. And know that a letter from you will do me good.

Ever yours, Vincent ✒

25

ANDY WHALE

Francis A. Schaeffer

❖

TO WIN AS MANY AS I CAN

I am sure "separation" is correct, but it is only one principle. There are others to be kept as well. The command to love should

---

Like C. S. Lewis, *Francis Schaeffer* is considered a leading 20th-century apologist among Christian fundamentalists. A Presbyterian pastor from America, he and his wife Edith settled in the Swiss Alps in 1948. Seven years later they started L'Abri, a retreat and study center for intellectuals and spiritual seekers.

Schaeffer wrote this letter to a friend in America in 1951. After recalling his earlier involvement in the Evangelical separatist movement, he tells about how his move to Europe has opened up a wider view of God and His people.

---

mean something. . . . [I am not suggesting that] I have learned to live in the light of Christ's command of love — first toward God, then the brethren, and then the lost. I know I have not. But I want to learn, and I know I must if I am to have that closeness to the Lord I wish to have. . . . God willing, I will push and politick no more. . . . The mountains are too high, history is too long, and eternity is longer. God is too great, man is too small, there are many of God's dear children, and all around there are men going to Hell. And if one man and a small group of men do not approve of where I am and what I do, does it prove I've missed success? No; only one thing will determine that — whether this day I'm where the Lord of lords and King of kings wants me to be. To win as many as I can, to help strengthen the hands of those who fight unbelief in the historical setting in which they are placed, to know the reality of "the Lord is my song," and to be committed to the Holy Spirit — that is what I wish I could know to be the reality of each day as it closes.

Have I learned all this? No, but I would not exchange that portion of it which I have, by God's grace, for all the hand-clapping I have had when I have been on the top of the pile. I have been a poor learner, but I'm further on than I was three years ago and I like it.

Jeffrey, I've seen the Holy Spirit work in individual lives like I have never experienced before. It reminds me of what I've heard of the revivals of yesterday. It would not be counted for much — only one's and two's — but it is as different as day and night from the way I've seen it come before. If the Lord can do it with me, with all I know is wrong with Schaeffer, with one's and two's, He can do it with hundreds too if He wishes. . . .

I know I've made mistakes and I know I've sinned. And where I know it, I have tried to make it right with those I have hurt, to confess it

OLI TENNENT

Gradually my thinking has changed - I have realized that in many things previously I have been mistaken.

to the Lord and try to follow His way. . . . My inclination is to think that Christ meant it in a very literal way when He said to seek the lower seats. That does not mean, as I see it, that we should refuse the higher if the Lord takes us there, but He should do the taking. I regret the times in my life when this has not been the case. . . .

Because of our past closeness [I have written these] seventeen pages of handwriting to you. The longest letter I have written — I think — since I was courting Edith ! . . .

Love from Edith to Hope, and from all of us to all of you our warmest greetings. I pray for you often and thank God for you. ➘

Francois de Salignac de la Moth Fenelon

❖

ON SILENCE AND RECOLLECTION

JAMES STRACHAN

I think, Madame, that you should try hard to learn to practice silence, so far as general courtesy will admit of. Silence promotes the Presence of God, avoids many harsh or proud words, and suppresses many dangers in the way of ridiculing or rashly judging our neighbors. Silence humbles the mind, and detaches it from the world; it would create a kind of solitude in the heart like that you court; it would supply much that you need under present difficulties.... You know very well that retirement is not essential to the love of God. When He gives you time, you must take it and use it; but meanwhile·abide patiently, satisfied that whatever He allots you is best. Lift up your heart to Him continually, without making any outward sign; only talk when it is necessary, and bear quietly with what crosses you. As you grow in the faith, God will treat you accordingly. You stand more in need of mortification than of light. The only thing I dread for you is dissipation; but you may remedy even that by silence. If you are steadfast in keeping silence when it is not necessary to speak, God will preserve

Lift up your heart to Him continually, without making any outward sign....

you from evil when it is right for you to talk.

If you are unable to secure much time to yourself, be all the more careful about stray moments. Even a few minutes gleaned faithfully amid engagements will be more profitable in God's Sight than whole hours given up to Him at freer seasons. Moreover, many brief spaces of time through the day will amount to something considerable at last. Possibly you yourself may find the advantage of such frequent recollection in God's Presence more than in a regular definite period allotted to devotion.

Your lot, Madame, is to love, to be silent, and to sacrifice your inclinations, in order to fulfill the Will of God by molding yourself to that of others. Happy indeed you are thus to bear a cross laid on you by God's Own Hands in the order of His Providence. The penitential work we choose, or even accept at the hands of others, does not so stifle self-love as that which God assigns us from day to day. In it we find nothing to foster self, and, coming as it does directly from His Merciful Providence, it

Your lot, Madame, is to love, to be silent, and to sacrifice....

brings with it grace sufficient for all our needs. All we have to do is to give ourselves up to God day by day, without looking further; He will carry us in His Arms as a loving mother carries her child. Let us believe, hope, love, with a child's simplicity, in every need looking with affection and trust to our Heavenly Father. He has said in His Own Word, "Can a woman forget her sucking child? . . . Yea, she may forget, yet will I not forget thee."

François de Salignac de la Moth Fénelon was born in 1651 and at the age of twelve sent to the Seminary of Saint Sulpice in Paris where he studied philosophy and theology. He began to preach when he was only fifteen and wished to go to Canada as a missionary. His superiors, however, felt he was not strong enough and instead he became the spiritual director of a community of women. His letters deal not only with the temptations Christians face, but with the forgiveness a loving God offers.

Wolfgang Amadeus Mozart

❖

THE GIFT OF CREATIVITY

When I am, as it were, completely myself, entirely alone, and of good cheer — say, travelling in a carriage, or walking after a good meal, or during the night when I cannot sleep; it is on such occasions that my ideas flow best and most abundantly. Whence and how they come, I know not; nor can I force them. Those ideas that please me I retain in memory, and am accustomed, as I have been told, to hum them to myself. If I continue in this way, it soon occurs to me how I may turn this or that morsel to account, so as to make a good dish of it, that is to say, agreeably to the rules of counterpoint, to the peculiarities of the various instruments, etc.

All this fires my soul, and, provided I am not disturbed, my subject enlarges itself, becomes methodized and defined, and the whole, though it be long, stands almost complete and finished in my mind, so that I can survey it,

> *All this fires my soul, and, provided I am not disturbed, my subject enlarges itself. . . .*

like a fine picture or a beautiful statue, at a glance. Nor do I hear in my imagination the parts successively, but I hear them, as it were, all at once. What a delight this is I cannot tell. All this inventing, this producing, takes place in a pleasing lively dream. Still the actual hearing of the *tout ensemble* is after all the best. What has been

This famous composer has become legendary, not only for his divine music but for his rare ability to tune in to the "voice of God" in his musical mind. In this letter, Mozart reveals his experience of inspiration as a creative flow from his Divine Maker.

thus produced I do not easily forget, and this is perhaps the best gift I have my Divine Maker to thank for.

  When I proceed to write down my ideas, I take out of the bag of my memory, if I may use that phrase, what has been previously collected into it in the way I have mentioned. For this reason the committing to paper is done quickly enough, for everything is, as I said before, already finished; and it rarely differs on paper from what it was in my imagination. At this occupation I can therefore suffer myself to be disturbed; for whatever may be going on around me, I write, and even talk, but only of fowls and geese, or of Gretel or Bärbel, or some such matters. But why my productions take from my hand that particular form and style that makes them *Mozartish*, and different from the works of other composers, is probably owing to the same cause which renders my nose so large or so aquiline, or, in short, makes it Mozart's, and different from those of other people. For I really do not study or aim at any originality. ➡

*Something happens to our thoughts
and emotions when we put them
into a letter; they are then not the
same as spoken words. They are
placed in a different, special context,
and they speak at a different level,
serving the soul's organ of
rumination rather than the mind's
capacity for understanding.*

—Thomas Moore

GEORGE SMITH, 1829–1901

MICHAEL ORTON

I wonder if I am true to Christ, if I have obeyed His will. I have obeyed man, all right. I am not so sure I have obeyed my Lord.

—From a letter to Dorothy Day

Thomas Merton

❖

A GREATER SCANDAL THAN WE THINK

Thank you for your last letter, and for the offer of Cassian. Yes, we can certainly use it. We do not have him in the novitiate, except some translations we ran off on a pale purple machine, which are not too legible. I am going to be lecturing on him shortly. Your offer is providential.

Perseverance — yes, more and more one sees that it is the great thing. But there is a thing that must not be overlooked. Perseverance is not hanging on to some course which we have set our minds to, and refusing to let go. It is not even a matter of getting a bulldog grip on the faith and not letting the devil pry us loose from it — though many of the saints

made it look that way. Really, there is something lacking in such a hope as that.
Hope is a greater scandal than we think. I am coming to think that God (may
He be praised in His great mystery) loves and helps best those who are so beat
and have so much nothing when they come to die that it is almost as if they had
persevered in nothing but had gradually lost everything, piece by piece, until
there was nothing left but God. Hence perseverance is not hanging on but
letting go. That of course is terrible. But as you say so rightly, it is a question of
His hanging on to us, by the hair of the head, that is from on top and beyond,
where we cannot see or reach. What man can see the top of his own head? If we
reach it — this we can do — we stand a good chance of interfering with God's
grip (may He forgive us).

O Dorothy, I think of you, and the beat
people, and the ones with nothing, and the
poor in virtue, the very poor, the ones no one
can respect. I am not worthy to say I love all
of you. Intercede for me, a stuffed shirt in a
place of stuffed shirts and a big dumb phony,
who have tried to be respectable and have succeeded. What a deception! I know, of course,
you are respected too, but you have a right to
be, and you didn't jump into the most respectable possible situation and then tell
everyone all about it. I am not worried about
all this and am not beating myself over the
head. I just think that for the love of God I
should say it, and that for the love of God you
should pray for me. . . . ✑

In 1941, when *Thomas Merton* decid-
ed to enter the monastery, he was
prepared to sacrifice his writing talents
for the contemplative life of a Trappist
monk. But his superiors insisted that
he keep on writing.

Although letter writing is not part of
the Trappist tradition, the quality of
writing in Merton's extensive correspondence almost rivals that of his published works. Few have succeeded as
Merton has, in writing serious letters
and making an art of it. This is an
excerpt from a letter written in 1960 to
Dorothy Day, who had recently started
the Catholic Worker soup kitchen
among the poor in New York's Lower
East Side.

Saint Jerome

— ❖ —

THE DESERT, FAIREST CITY OF ALL

Oh how I wish I were now present in your community and — though these eyes of mine are unworthy to behold — to share with all enthusiasm your wonderful fellowship! I would then be gazing upon the desert, the fairest city of all. I would be seeing places deserted by their inhabit-

This 4th-century biblical scholar and Doctor of the Church was eager to further the cause of asceticism in the Early Church after he had a dream in which a heavenly judge accused him of worldliness. Jerome left the "world" of Antioch to join the anchorites in northern Syria. Later he founded a monastery in Bethlehem.

This letter was written in the autumn of 374, shortly before Jerome's decision to become a hermit.

ants thronged by bands of saints — a veritable paradise.

But since my sins keep my person, beset by every form of transgression, from becoming a member of your blessed society, therefore I beseech you — and I have no doubt that you can do it — that by your prayers you set me free from the darkness of this world. I have told you this before when I was with you, and now by way of letter I mention to you again my ardent desire; for my mind and heart are un-

I beseech you, that by your prayers you set me free from the darkness of this world.

alterably set on its achievement. It is for you, then, to see that success follows my resolve. My part is to show the will; it is that of your prayers that I have the power as well as the will.

I am like the sick sheep that strays from the rest of the flock. Unless the Good Shepherd takes me on His shoulders and carries me back to His fold, my steps will falter, and in the very effort of rising my feet will give way. I am that prodigal son who wasted all the portion entrusted to me by my father. But I have not yet fallen at my father's knees. I have not yet begun to put away from me the enticements of my former riotous living.

And because I have not so much given up my sins as begun to wish a little to give them up, now the devil is trying to ensnare me in new nets. He puts new stumbling blocks in my way, he encompasses me on every side with the ocean's waters and on every side with the ocean's deep. I find myself in the midst of the element, unwilling to retreat and unable to advance. It remains that through your prayers the breath of the Holy Spirit waft me onward and bring me to the haven of the longed-for shore. ━●

For what is there so present, to put it that way, when we are absent from each other, as to be able to speak to and to hear those you love through correspondance?

—From a letter to Niceas

CHRIS HARVEY

ANDY WHALE

RENÉ HARTZNER

If we turn our back on them, we turn it on Christ, and at the hour of our death we will be judged if we have recognized Christ in them, and what we have done for and to them.

—From a letter
to her co-workers

38

A BETTER CRIB

My Dearest Children,

This year we must prepare a better crib, a crib of poverty. It will be easy to fill the emptiness of the crib with charity.

We think we know ourselves enough. Our very lives are all for God, therefore why spend so much time on our spiritual life? It is not that we do not make our examen; no, we do it but do it alone. We have to do it with Christ if we want to make it real. Jesus is our co-worker.

Our souls should be like a clear glass through which God can be seen. Often this glass becomes spotted with dust and dirt. To remove this dirt and dust we make our examen, so that we become once more "clean of heart." He can, and He will help us to remove the "dirt and dust" if we allow Him to do it, with a sincere will to let Him have His way. Perhaps something has been lacking in us. Our vows, our duties, the virtues, our attitude to and our contacts with our neighbors . . . provide us with food enough for reflection. If we examine ourselves and find nothing to engage our attention, we need Jesus to help us detect our infidelities.

Our examen is after all the mirror we hold up to our nature, a poor weak human nature, no doubt, but one that needs the mirror to reflect faithfully all its deficiencies. If we undertake this work more sincerely, perhaps we shall find what we thought were stumbling blocks transformed by Him into stepping stones.

Agnes Bojaxhiu of Macedonia, now known as Mother Teresa of Calcutta, is a living testimony of God's love put into action. Since she arrived in Calcutta in 1931, the order she founded has grown to 3,000 sisters and 537 houses serving the poorest of the poor in 114 countries.

Mother Teresa wrote this Christmas letter of instruction to her Sisters in 1963.

Lev Tolstoy

❖

THE IMPORTANT THING THAT UNITES US

lexandrine, my dear, kind, old friend,

Tanya Kuzminskaya wrote to me about you and about your illness (I thank her for it) — that you are very weak and, in our human judgement, apparently close to death. I too was very close to it, but here I am still not dead, and sometimes I regret it — it was so good to be dying — will it be like that another time? — but sometimes I'm glad because I think that our senile lives are not only not useless, as people often think, but on the contrary, are of the utmost importance in terms of the influence that old people can exert on others. You, with your ardent religious feeling and heart of gold, have probably experienced and are experiencing the enlightenment that illness gives, and are now more than ever before, not just probably, but certainly, spreading love and goodness round about you. I'm writing this letter only so as to tell you how often in my relations with you I have felt this love and goodness of yours, and feeling it, have become better myself. I also want to tell you that you're mistaken in thinking — if

Count *Lev Nikolaevich Tolstoy*, 19th-century Russian philosopher, mystic and novelist, wrote more than 10,000 letters. His correspondence with Countess Alexandra Tolstaya particularly illustrates his maturing spiritual sensibility.

Toward the end of his life, Tolstoy gained the almost prophetic role of Christian anarchist, and had many followers throughout Europe. However, Tolstoy renounced organized "Tolstoyism," and all worldly goods (including his estate) in order to seek the kingdom of God through love and the ascetic struggle for perfection.

Tolstoy wrote this letter to Alexandra in 1903. Alexandra died shortly afterwards.

you do think — that you and I are separated by our faith. My faith and your faith and the faith of all good people (forgive me for the immodesty of including myself among them) are one and the same thing: faith in God the Father, who sent us into this world to do His will. His will is that we should love each other and do to others as we would have them do to us. And the fact that I have carried out His will badly and am still carrying it out badly now doesn't frighten me, since I know that God is love and that He knows I have tried, especially just recently, to carry out His will, and not from fear of punishment but because the more I have done His will, the better my life has always been. And I'm sure you believe exactly the same. But even if I don't believe in some details you believe in, I don't think it's important and can't separate us in view of the very important thing that unites us.

This expressed everything I felt, and comforted and cheered me.

When I was very close to death, and my thoughts refused to function, and I tried to express my attitude towards the impending passage from this life to the other, I remember I found only one thought, one feeling, one appeal to God; I said to myself: *from Thee I came and unto Thee I shall return*. And this expressed everything I felt and comforted and cheered me. I'm sure that you feel the same, and this feeling again unites us.

If they read this letter of mine to you, tell them to write me a couple of lines about how you feel and whether things are well with you.

Goodbye, for now, my dear; be assured of my sincere love for you and my gratitude for all the good you have given me during the half century of our friendship. ☙

There is (a) kind of simplicity that is soulful: using plain, frank language, speaking directly about emotions and situations, allowing oneself to be transparent and visible. These simple forms of expression allow the soul to be seen, and are therefore valuable in letter writing.

—Thomas Moore

JOHANN GEORG MEYER VON BREMEN, 1813–86

Henry David Thoreau

❖

THE RIGHT TO GRIEVE

Dear Friend,

I believe I have nothing new to tell you, for what was news you have learned from other sources. I am much the same person that I was, who should be so much better; yet when I realize what has transpired, and the greatness of the part I am unconsciously acting, I am thrilled and it seems as if there were now a history to match it.

Soon after John's death I listened to a music-box, and if, at any time, that even had seemed inconsistent with the beauty and harmony of the universe, it was then gently constrained into the placid course of nature by those steady notes, in mild and unoffended tone echoing far and wide under the heavens. But I find these things more strange than sad to me. What right have I to grieve, who have not ceased to wonder?

What right have I to grieve, who have not ceased to wonder?

We feel at first as if some opportunities of kindness and sympathy were lost, but learn afterward that any pure grief is ample recompense for all. That is, if we are faithful; for a spent grief is but sympathy with

Henry David Thoreau, great American naturalist and author of *Walden*, had suddenly lost his brother John when he wrote this letter. Mrs. Lucy Brown was a sister-in-law to his friend Emerson, who had just lost his son Waldo (Thoreau's favorite) a month earlier. In this letter of 1842 to Mrs. Brown, Thoreau expresses his sorrow and hope.

MICHAEL ORTON

the soul that disposes events, and is as natural as the resin of Arabian trees. Only nature has a right to

For we are not what we are, nor do we treat or esteem each other for such, but for what we are capable of being.

grieve perpetually, for she only is innocent. Soon the ice will melt, and the blackbirds sing along the river which he frequented, as pleasantly as ever. The same everlasting serenity will appear in this face of God, and we will not be sorrowful, if he is not.

We are made happy when reason can discover no occasion for it. The memory of some past moments is more persuasive than the experience of present ones. There have been visions of such breadth and brightness that these motes were invisible in their light.

I do not wish to see John ever again – I mean him who is dead – but that other whom only he would have wished to see, or to be, of whom he was the imperfect representative. For we are not what we are, nor do we treat or esteem each other for such, but for what we are capable of being. As for Waldo, he died as the mist rises from the brook, which the sun will soon dart his rays through. Do not the flowers die every autumn? He had not even taken root here. I was not startled to hear that he was dead; it seemed the most natural event that could happen. His fine organization demanded it, and nature gently yielded its request. It would have been strange if he had lived. Neither will nature manifest any sorrow at his death, but soon the note of the lark will be heard down in the meadow, and fresh dandelions will spring from the old stocks where he plucked them last summer. I have been living ill of late, but am now doing better. How do you live in that Plymouth world, now-a-days? Please remember me to Mary Russell. You must not blame me if I do talk to the clouds, for I remain. ✒

Ludwig van Beethoven

❖

CHRISTIAN DELIGHTS

I call thee "thou!" Surely thou wilt forgive me! I cannot forsake thee even though thou art a Jewess! Holy Writ knows the names of thy people's men, it tells of the bril-

Oh, why does not all mankind stand united in the fold of the Redeemer?

liant deeds they have done. But I turned my eyes and saw in the depths of my heart the sanctuary of my temple: The Savior!

Oh, why does not all mankind stand united in the fold of the Redeemer? What devastation is here on earth — and how envious a destiny has hurled all us human beings into ruins and darkness!

Rahel, beloved creature, for the sake of my tender solicitude, acknowledge the Redeemer's lordship, for his name becomes more glorious on earth from generation to generation!

No mercy is felt for thy people: the parson's word always calls back the past. Turn thy heart to the Savior, and in stillness build up the treasures of experience! Suffering is the happiness of thy people: be mine, and come to know delights, Christian delights! ✒

Among *Beethoven's* many loves and letters, this one stands out for its peculiar bluntness. In 1792, the 22-year-old German composer met Rahel Löwenstein, a lovely 17-year-old girl. When he found out she was Jewish, he wrote her this impassioned letter. The letter did not have the desired result, and the relationship ended a month later.

Corrie ten Boom

❖

FORGIVEN

Dear Sir,
Today I heard that most probably you are the one who betrayed me. I went through 10 months of concentration camp. My father died after 9 days of imprisonment. My sister died in prison, too.

I have forgiven you everything. God will also forgive you everything, if you ask Him.

The harm you planned was turned into good for me by God. I came nearer to Him. A severe punishment is awaiting you. I have prayed for you, that the Lord may accept you if you will repent. Think that the Lord Jesus on the Cross also took your sins upon Himself. If you accept this and want to be His child, you are saved for Eternity.

I have forgiven you everything. God will also forgive you everything, if you ask Him. He loves you and He Himself sent His Son to earth to reconcile your sins, which meant to suffer the punishment for you and me. You, on your part have to give an answer to this. . . . If it is difficult for you to pray, then ask if God will give you His Spirit, who works the faith in your heart.

Never doubt the Lord Jesus' love. He is standing with His arms spread out to receive you.

I hope that the path which you will now take may work for your eternal salvation. ⌐

This Dutch woman is known to Christians all over the world for her book *The Hiding Place*, an account of her life in The Netherlands and in Ravensbrück concentration camp during World War II. The message of love and forgiveness which she passed on to the world is illustrated in this letter. She wrote it after her release in 1944 to the person who betrayed her to the Nazis.

MICHAEL ORTON

MICHAEL ORTON

David Livingstone

❖

A FATHER'S ADVICE

I have been so busy writing despatches of late that I have been unable to write to you, though it has frequently been in my mind that I ought to try. We have had but little intercourse . . . and while I was in England I was so busy that I could not enjoy much the company of my children. I am still as busy and believe I am doing good service to the cause of Christ on earth. He is pleased to crown my efforts with a sort of success that the world applauds . . . but I long to see the time approaching when the long degraded sons of Africa will stretch out their hands to God. You will understand this if I tell you that we have just returned from the discovery of a magnificent lake called Shirwa. . . .

This great Scottish missionary and explorer, who opened up Africa to missionary work and western civilization, rarely was able to spend time with his children due to his many expeditions. This letter written in 1859 to his son Robert in England shows a father's concern for his teenage son. Robert eventually went to America and died as a soldier in the Civil War.

As one individual I can do nothing, but God has put it in my heart to try, and He has helped me, and every time He enables me by a discovery or otherwise to bring the subject before men's minds He is helping. Our great duty as His children is to work with Him and for Him. It often seems slow work, aye, and not at all unlikely that I shall lie down and die before my desires for England and Africa are half accomplished. But if I work faithfully He will not be unmindful of the work of faith and labour of love. . . .

Don't try to be anything else than what you are. Never look to others and imagine that to be a servant of Christ you must be like them.

I wish you to be a thankful loving child of God. You must give yourself just as you are to Him. Don't try to be anything else but what you are. Never look at others and imagine that to be a servant of Christ you must be like them. Make an entire surrender of your whole nature to God. Give yourself to Him to be what He wills you to be, and look to Jesus and to Him alone as your pattern, your wisdom, your righteousness, your sanctification, your redemption. He has much work to do and He needs people of various capacities and tempers to do it. If you give yourself to Him, He will employ you honorably in life, and in death you will not be unlamented. You must choose some walk in life with a distinct reference to God's glory among men. It is a mistake to suppose that God is best served in the ministry. I serve Him now in command of a steamer. I can ask God's blessing to rest upon me on the paddle-box with as good a conscience as I should were I in other circumstances ascending the pulpit. Choose a path by which you will be able by your exertions to benefit the world, and bend your energies to that, and may the Almighty God grant you His directing aid. . . .

Choose a path . . . and bend your energies to that.

*Under how great
obligation then are
we, living in a world
civilized by the arts,
not to discontinue
(the) practice
(of letter writing)?*

—St. Jerome

MASTER OF THE FEMALE HALF LENGTHS, C.1550

Flannery O'Connor

❖

STRUGGLING WITH FAITH

As a freshman in college you are bombarded with new ideas, or rather pieces of ideas, new frames of reference, an activation of the intellectual life which is only beginning, but which is already running ahead of your lived experience. After a year of this, you think you cannot believe. You are just beginning

This novelist and short-story writer is one of the finest in 20th-century American literature. Though filled with grotesque characters and bizarre settings, O'Connor's writing is profoundly moral, stressing the reality of sin and the glory of redemption.

O'Connor wrote this letter to a college student who had heard her lecture in May 1962. It encourages the reader to deal with doubt in an honest way.

to realize how difficult it is to have faith and the measure of a commitment to it, but you are too young to decide you don't have faith just because you feel you cannot believe. . . . One result of the stimulation of your intellectual life that takes place in college is usually a shrinking of the imaginative life. This sounds like a paradox, but I have often found it to be true. Students get so bound up with difficulties . . . that they cease to look for

Where you have absolute solutions, you have no need of faith.

God in other ways. Bridges once wrote Gerard Manley Hopkins and asked him to tell him how he, Bridges, could believe. He must have expected from Hopkins a long philosophical answer. Hopkins wrote back, "Give alms." He was trying to say to Bridges that God is to be experienced in Charity (in the sense of love for the divine image in human beings). Don't get so entangled with intellectual difficulties that you fail to look for God in this way.

The intellectual difficulties have to be met, however, and you will be meeting them for the rest of your life. When you get a reasonable hold on one, another will come to take its place. At one time, the clash of the different world religions was a difficulty for me. Where you have absolute solutions, however, you have no need of faith. Faith is what you have in the absence of knowledge. The reason this clash doesn't bother me any longer is because I have got, over the years, a sense of the immense sweep of creation, of the evolutionary process in everything, of how incomprehensible God must necessarily be to be the God of heaven and earth. . . .

If you want your faith, you have to work for it. It is a gift, but for very few it is a gift given without any demand for equal time devoted to its cultivation. For every book you read that is anti-Christian, make it your business to read one that presents the other side of the picture; if one isn't satisfactory read others. Don't think that you have to abandon reason to be a Christian. . . .

Even in the life of a Christian, faith rises and falls like the tides of an invisible sea.

Even in the life of a Christian, faith rises and falls like the tides of an invisible sea. It's there, even when he can't see it or feel it, if he wants it to be there. You realize, I think, that it is more valuable, more mysterious, altogether more immense than anything you can learn or decide upon in college. Learn what you can, but cultivate Christian scepticism. It will keep you free – not free to do anything you please, but free to be formed by something larger than your own intellect or the intellects of those around you.

I don't know if this is the kind of answer that can help you, but any time you care to write me, I can try to do better. ━●

THE GRANDEUR OF THE HUMAN SOUL

Today I made the ascent of the highest mountain of this district, which is not unfitly called "Ventoux" [Windy], induced by the single desire of seeing the remarkable height of the place. I have had this expedition in mind for many years. For from my infancy, as you know, I have haunted this region through the fate which haunts human affairs; and this mountain, conspicuous from all quarters, is almost always in view. At length an impulse seized me to accomplish at once what I was always purposing. . . .

On the appointed day we [Petrarch and his brother] left our home, and arrived at dusk at Malaucene, a place lying under the northern face of the mountain. After staying there a day, we at length, taking a servant apiece, ascended the peak today with a good deal of difficulty. It is a precipitous and inaccessible mass of rocky ground; but as the poet well says: "Relentless toil conquers all." The day was long, the weather was kind; we

JOHN TURNER

Petrarch has been called "the first modern man" and "the morning star of the Renaissance." In this letter written in 1336 to his confessor, Father Dionisio Roberti, Petrarch tells about his ascent of Mount Ventoux, a 64,000-foot peak near Avignon, and relates his experience to the spiritual quest of the human soul.

all had such gifts as strength of mind and vigorous activity of body; our sole hindrance was the steep and trackless route. On the lower folds of the mountain we met an old shepherd, who tried hard to dissuade us from the ascent, saying that fifty years before, in an excess of youthful ardor like our own, he had himself reached the top, and had gained nothing from it but repentance and toil, a body bruised and clothes torn with rocks and briars, and that he had never, either before or since that time, heard of anyone who had dared the like.

While he shouted all this to us, our desire to proceed was increased by his dissuasion, for young men put no faith in such warnings. So, when the old man saw his efforts were in vain, he went a little way with us and pointed out a steep path among the cliffs, giving us much good advice and continuing it, even after we had part-

Many doubtful and difficult struggles lie before me! What I used to love, I love no longer — nay, I lie, I do love, but with more restraint, more moderately, more regretfully.

ed from him. Before he went off we left with him such garments and other things as impeded us, and grappled with the single task of the ascent, mounting up with eagerness. But, as often happens, the mighty effort was soon followed by fatigue; so, not far from there, we rested on a crag. . . .

I sat down in a kind of dell. There, passing in swift thought from the corporeal to the spiritual, I addressed myself in words like these: Rest assured that what thou hast so often experienced today in climbing this mountain happens to thyself and many who strive after the blessed life. And the reason why men do not so clearly perceive it is that the movements of the body are in the open, while those of the soul are unseen and hidden. Indeed, the blessed life, as we call it, is situated on a lofty summit, and "narrow is the way" that leads thereto. . . .

The highest summit of all is that which the woodsmen call "The Little Son" — why I know not, unless, like so many other things, it be by antiphrasis, for it seems the father of all the neighboring heights. On its top there is a small level space, where at last we rested our weary limbs. . . . I stood as one dazed. I looked back; the clouds were beneath my feet. . . .

While I marveled at these things in turn, now recognizing some earthly object, now lifting my soul upwards as my body had been, I thought of looking at the book of Augustine's *Confessions*, the gift of your love — which I never forget for the sake both of author and giver, and which I always have with me. I opened the little volume, of handy size but of infinite charm, in order to read whatever met my eye, for nothing could meet it but what was pious and devout. I opened it by chance at the tenth book, while my brother stood intent, expect-ing to hear Augustine speak by my mouth. I call God to witness, and my listener too, that these were the words on which my eyes fell: "Men go abroad to admire the heights of mountains, and the mighty billows, and the long-winding courses of rivers — the compass of the ocean and the courses of the stars — and themselves they neglect."

I confess I was amazed; and begging my brother, who was eager to hear more, not to trouble me, I closed the book, indignant with myself that at that very moment I was admiring earthly things — I, who ought to have learnt long ago from even heathen philosophers that there is nothing admirable but the soul — in itself so great that nothing can be great beside it. Then indeed, content with what I had seen from the mountain, I turned my eyes inwardly upon myself, and from that moment none heard me say a word till we reached the bottom. . . .

> *The movements of the body are in the open, while those of the soul are unseen and hidden. Indeed, the blessed life, as we call it, is situated on a lofty summit, and narrow is the way that leads thereto.*

I pondered in silence on the poverty of men's designs, who, neglecting the noblest part of their being and seeking without what could be found within, spend themselves in countless things, and waste their strength on empty shows. I thought with amazement of the grandeur of the human soul. . . .

This, too, came into my mind at every step; if we freely undergo such sweat and toil in order to raise the body a little nearer heaven, what cross or prison or sting should keep the soul from approaching to God, and from rising superior to the summits of pride and the doom of death! And I thought how few are not diverted from this path either by the fear of hardship or the desire of comfort. . . . How earnestly should we strive — not to stand on lofty spots on earth, but to have beneath our feet the appetites that spring from earthly impulses! . . .

Pray, I beg you, that these thoughts, so long wandering and unsettled, may soon become firmly fixed; and that after long and aimless employment on many subjects, they may be turned to the one true, sure, enduring good. Farewell. ➳

JOHN TURNER

A letter is a mutual conversation between absent friends, which should be neither unpolished, rough, nor artificial, nor confined to a single topic, nor tediously long. Thus the epistolary form favors simplicity, frankness, humor, and wit.

—Erasmus of Rotterdam

CLAUDE ANDREW CALTHROP, 1845-93

DARRELL GULIN

Hudson Taylor

❖

THE AGONY OF SOUL

My own dear Sister — so many thanks for your long dear letter. . . . I do not think you have written me such a letter since we have been in China. I know it is with you as with me – you cannot, not you *will*

The last month or more has been, perhaps, the happiest of my life; and I long to tell you a little of what the Lord has done for my soul.

not. Mind and body will not bear more than a certain amount of strain, or do more than a certain amount of work. As to work, mine was never so

When *Hudson Taylor* landed in Shanghai in 1854, he began a fifty-year long missionary ministry which would open mainland China to the Gospel of Christ. A visionary and hard-working man, Taylor was often tempted to go beyond God's leading. All his life he struggled with his impatient heart and strong will.

He wrote this letter, which is reprinted in parts, to his sister Amelia in 1869. In the letter he enthusiastically tells her of his newfound trust in God.

plentiful, so responsible, or so difficult; but the weight and strain are all gone. The last month or more has been, perhaps, the happiest of my life; and I long to tell you a little of what the Lord has done for my soul. . . .

My mind has been greatly exercised for six or eight months past, feeling the need personally, and for our Mission, of more holiness, life, power in our souls. But personal need stood first and was the greatest. I felt the ingratitude, the danger, the sin of not living nearer to God. . . . I knew that if I could only abide in Christ all would be well, but I *could not*. . . . Instead of growing stronger, I seemed to be getting weaker and to have less power against sin. . . .

When my agony of soul was at its height, a sentence in a letter from dear McCarthy was used to remove the scales from my eyes, and the Spirit of God revealed the truth of *our oneness* with *Jesus* as I had never known it before. McCarthy . . . wrote (I quote from memory):

"But how to get faith strengthened? Not by striving after faith, but by resting on the Faithful One."

As I read I saw it all! "If we believe *not*, he abideth faithful." I looked to Jesus and saw . . . that He had said, "*I* will never leave *you*." "Ah, *there* is rest!" I thought. "I have striven in vain to rest in Him. I'll strive no more. For has He not promised to abide with me – never to leave me,

But how to get faith strengthened? Not by striving after faith, but by resting on the Faithful One.

never to fail me?" And, dearie, *He never will!* . . . I am no longer anxious about anything, as I realize this; for He, I know, is able to carry out *His Will*, and His will is mine. . . .

I am no better than before (may I not say, in a sense, I do not wish to be, nor am I striving to be); but I am dead and buried with Christ – aye, and risen too and ascended; and now Christ lives in me. . . .

Etty Hillesum

❖

DIALOGUE WITH GOD

Darling Tide,
I thought at first I would give my writing a miss today because I'm so terribly tired and also because I thought I had nothing to say just now.

Etty Hillesum was a Dutch Jewess who worked at Westerbork, a Nazi transit camp on the border between The Netherlands and Germany. From there the Nazis deported Jews to Auschwitz. After her death in Auschwitz in 1943, her diaries were discovered and published in 1981. The book is considered by Jews and Chris-tians alike as the work of a great, modern mystic. It is the remarkable account of a woman's religious sensibility and dialogue with God.

This letter was written to a friend less than a month before Etty was deported to Auschwitz.

But of course I have a great deal to write about. I shall allow my thoughts free rein; you are bound to pick them up anyway. This afternoon I was resting on my bunk and suddenly I just had to write these few words in my diary, and I now send them to you: "You have made me so rich, oh God,

Things come and go in a deeper rhythm and people must be taught to listen to it, it is the most important thing we have to learn in this life.

please let me share Your beauty with open hands. My life has become an uninterrupted dialogue with You, oh God, one great dialogue. Sometimes when I stand in some corner of the camp, my feet planted on Your earth, my eyes raised towards Your Heaven, tears sometimes run down my face, tears of deep emotion and gratitude. At night, too, when I lie in my bed and rest in You, oh God, tears of grat-itude run down my face, and that is my prayer. I have been terribly tired for several days, but that, too, will pass; things come and go in a deeper rhythm and people must be taught to listen to it, it is the most important thing we have to learn in this life. I am not challenging You, oh God, my life is one great dialogue with You. I may never become the great artist I would really like to be, but I am already secure in You, God. Sometimes I try my hand at turning out small profundities and uncertain short stories, but I always end up with just one single word: God. And that says everything and there is no need for anything more. And all my creative powers are translated into inner dia-logues with You; the beat of my heart has grown deeper, more active and yet more peaceful, and it is as if I were all the time storing up inner riches."

There are many miracles in a human life, my own is one long sequence of inner miracles, and it's good to be able to say so again to somebody. Your photograph is in Rilke's Book of Hours, next to Jul's photograph, they lie under my pillow together with my small Bible. Your letter with the quotations has also arrived. Keep writing, please, and fare you well, my dear. ✒

God, my creative powers are translated into inner dialogues with You.

FRANK HERHOLDT

65

John Wesley

❖

BY SIMPLE FAITH

Dear Sister Bennis,

When you write to me, you have only to "think aloud," just to open the window in your breast. When we love one another, there is no need of either disguise or reserve. I love you, and I verily believe you love me; so you have only to write just what you feel.

The essential part of Christian holiness is giving the heart wholly to

God; and certainly we need not lose any degree of that light and love which at first attend this: it is our own infirmity if we do; it is not the will of the Lord concerning us. Your present business is not to reason whether you should call your experience thus or thus, but to go straight to Him that loves you, with all your wants, how great or how many soever they are. Then all things are ready; help, while you ask, is given. You have only to receive it by simple faith. Nevertheless you will still be encom-

You live in a house of clay, and therefore this corruptible body will more or less press down the soul.

passed with numberless infirmities; for you live in a house of clay, and therefore this corruptible body will more or less press down the soul, yet not so as to prevent your rejoicing evermore and having a witness that your heart is all His. You may claim this: it is yours; for Christ is yours. Believe, and feel Him near. ❧

John Wesley's profound religious experience led him to become the foremost leader and theologian of the Methodist tradition. Together with his brother Charles he transformed the spiritual climate in England during the 18th century. In this letter written in 1767, Wesley counsels a woman on Christian holiness.

*In our letters we are
recollecting and conversing
with the soul, through both
our friends and ourselves.*

—Thomas Moore

THOMAS FAED, 1826-1900

PAUL GREBLIUNAS

The best letters are those that were never published.

—Virginia Woolf